VITA WORE PANTS

The Story of a Mexican Freedom Fighter

by AIDA SALAZAR
Art by MOLLY MENDOZA

SCHOLASTIC PRESS
NEW YORK

JOVITA

dreamed of wearing pants
like her brothers, Ramón
and Luciano.

As was expected in rural Mexico in the 1910s, Abuela made Jovita and her sisters wear big skirts. Jovita hated the way they tangled like weeds around her legs as she scaled the tallest mesquite tree in Rancho Palos Blancos.

She wanted to ride Morongo and feel the wind curl her face into a smile.

Each morning, Jovita snuck out to tend the animals on the rancho and race Ramón. When she was well out of sight, she tucked her skirts into her bloomers. With her makeshift pants, Jovita could leap and easily outrun her brother.

Together, they explored the campo. Jovita discovered the way leaves rustle when rain is coming, where healing plants grow, the shape of every cave, and what might lurk inside: scorpions, coyotes, wolves, rattlers. She followed the rollicking rivers that gave fish and clean water. She listened to the songs of the cenzontles and mourning doves — a gentle *coo-coo-roo*-ing.

As Jovita grew, she heard whispers of a revolution in Mexico. The government had made laws that took power away from the Catholic Church and prevented people from practicing religion freely. Papá joined the Cristeros, the revolutionaries fighting for their rights against the Federation, and rode into the sierra with Luciano and Ramón.

Jovita was left behind, but she dreamed of accompanying her father and brothers and riding Morongo toward freedom.

One day, when Jovita was out with her abuela and sisters, government soldiers came to Palos Blancos in a fiery rage. The family returned home to find ashes where their house had been and the barn still smoking.

Jovita rushed Abuela and her sisters to the caves she knew so well. As soon as it was safe, they moved to another rancho, where Jovita formed a plan.

Of course, Jovita would make a good soldier. She was wise about the countryside, could ride better than most men, and was not afraid.

The next time Papá returned from the battlefield, she made her case.

Papá agreed to take
Jovita, but only to
observe. He would never
let her fire a shot or wear
pants. Jovita memorized Papá's
strategies as they sat by the
campfire eating what they'd hunted.
Beneath a blanket of shimmering
stars, she understood that la Sierra de
Morones would always be their friend.

When Jovita was fifteen, government soldiers captured her and demanded information about Papá. No matter how they hurt her, she stayed as strong as the mountain and did not give him up.

With the stealth of a fox, Jovita escaped into the moonlight, finding her way home to Abuela, guided by the silvery shadows of the sierra she knew so well.

Then, one terrible day, soon after Jovita returned home, the government killed Luciano. In her sadness, Jovita pushed again to become a soldier, but Papá refused. Jovita, her sisters, and Abuela were scattered like pollen across Mexico, forced to live with different relatives so they could be safe.

After a few years, the family reunited and the fighting calmed. Religion was practiced freely once more, but old war grudges remained. The government, still mad at Papá and his revolutionaries, found Papá and Ramón and engulfed them in a storm of bullets. Jovita never saw them alive again.

Sorrow swirled inside Jovita's heart.
Her sadness found sympathy with other
Cristeros, who met one evening to form
a plan for justice.

When she returned, Jovita cut her long hair short.
Next, she put on Ramón's cotton shirt, overalls,
riding boots, and wide-brimmed straw hat. Jovita was
reborn as a pants-wearing coronel named Juan. She
was ready to reignite the revolution.

Juan rode into la Sierra de Morones with eighty soldiers and her dog. Her soldiers agreed, if the government could kill Cristeros during a time of peace, their right to practice religion was still not safe. Juan would lead them to victory.

Juan knew where to graze their horses in every green, grassy field and how to find the mesas so big they shot straight up to touch the sky. She could close her eyes and name every spring that grew out of the earth and the ways the rivers and streams wrapped like necklaces along the mountains. As Juan, Jovita could finally wear pants while breathing in the clean sierra morning air, ready to fulfill her mission of justice.

Jovita's peasant army fought dangerous battles against the powerful government. Her skills were sharp. She listened closely to her dog's warnings that the enemy was near, and rode flat on her belly while shooting. Her knowledge of the secrets of the land helped them win or escape each time.

They fought hard for six years, and finally the Federation offered Jovita a truce. She weighed her options and thought of her loved ones. She had won many battles but had also seen the loss of many lives. Jovita decided to surrender peacefully to the government.

Word of Jovita's courage spread like wildfire across the sierra. She had become so well-known that a songwriter composed a corrido in her honor. President Cárdenas insisted on meeting the coronel who had given them such a hard time on the battlefield.

Jovita strode out of that room a proud revolutionary fighter. She had surrendered one battle but won another. She wore a wide-brimmed hat, a long-sleeved cotton shirt, riding boots, and a crisp pair of new blue jeans.

She wore them well, like she'd always dreamed.

MORE ABOUT
JOVITA

Jovita Valdovinos was born on February 24, 1911, in Rancho Palos Blancos in the municipality of Jalpa, Zacatecas, Mexico, the sixth and youngest child of Maria Elena Medina Pedroza and Teófilo Valdovinos. Her mother died when she was only one year old, and her father let her maternal grandmother, Ramona Pedroza, take charge of raising her and her siblings. Jovita spent her childhood tending the farm animals and roaming the countryside with her favorite brother, Ramón, despite her community's traditional gender expectations.

When the Mexican Revolution for land reform of 1910–1920 ended, a new socialist government was installed. Their new constitution severely restricted the power of the Catholic Church. They outlawed religious teaching by the Church and put Church property in control of the Mexican government. In 1925, President Calles used his army to enforce these restrictions, which led priests to abandon their churches. The state took possession of parochial schools, redistributed Catholic-owned lands, and killed priests and religious practitioners. However,

Jovita Valdovinos wearing traditional denim overalls, long-sleeved shirt, and riding boots, holding a wide-brimmed hat, on the day of her surrender to the government, August 1935.

After the war, Jovita continued to wear pants. Shown here, she is out for the evening wearing jeans and a long-sleeved shirt with a handkerchief, or pañuelo, around her neck.

many of the rural poor in the Mexican states of Zacatecas, Jalisco, Durango, and Michoacan sought to challenge these restrictions and rose up in arms to fight for their religious rights. This resistance was the beginning of the first wave of the Cristero Revolution.

Jovita's father, Teófilo Valdovinos, commanded a battalion of men, most of whom lived in pueblos and rural communities near Jalpa, Zacatecas. They were underfunded and less armed than the government forces, also called the Federation.

In 1925, when Jovita was fourteen, her father and brothers' participation in the Cristero Revolution took a deep personal toll. Her family's home was burned to the ground, and they were forced to live in caves. Jovita was captured by the Federales because they thought she would give up the whereabouts of her family. Though she was beaten and assaulted over the course of several months, she remained loyal to her family and did not expose them. When she tried to escape, she was shot in the arm and chest but survived. After Jovita spent seven days on bed rest, the Federales let down their guard, and she escaped, stealing thousands of pesos from the general who had assaulted her and held her captive. Soon after, her brother Luciano was killed. Her capture and Luciano's death sowed in Jovita a deep-seeded resentment against the Federales.

Other, noncombatant women supporters of the Cristeros called themselves the Feminine Brigades of Joan of Arc. Their group was an important source of civilian support for the Cristero Revolution, with nearly 25,000 members.

Jovita wanted to do more than other women, some of whom became religious leaders. She wanted to fight. Her father refused to let her but did take Jovita with him into the Sierra de Morones. There she learned to be a soldier. However, her father was loyal to the gender roles of the time and did not allow her to shoot during battle or to dress like a man.

Though the fighting calmed after the first wave of the Cristero Revolution, the government sought revenge against former revolutionaries. In 1930, Jovita's brother Ramón and her father were killed by the Federation in a bloody shootout. Grief was the fuel that propelled Jovita to take up arms to avenge the deaths of her father, brothers, and other revolutionaries and ignite the second wave of the Cristero Revolution.

Jovita changed her name to "Juan" and cut her hair short. She took on the typical dress for peasant men — denim overalls, a long-sleeved cotton shirt, and a wide-brimmed straw hat. Because of the legacy her father left her and her command of the ways of the countryside, eighty men followed her into battle to claim justice for the revolutionaries.

As a coronel, Jovita led her battalion through the Sierra de Morones while riding a prized stallion. The sierra's topography was rugged and bewildering to the Federation but intimately familiar to Jovita. She emerged as a clever war strategist against the Federation. Jovita also relied on the barking of her dog, El Africano, who alerted them when the enemy approached. She loved her dog dearly and had special huaraches, or sandals, made to protect his paws. In addition,

A family of Cristeros pose with rifles. There was little-known female involvement in the armed struggle. Women were expected to provide support for the troops (caretaking, cooking, farming, and sometimes smuggling money and arms), all while wearing the customary skirts.

Cristeros in the Sierra de Morones. While not Jovita's troupe, this group, in traditional clothes of the era, is typical of those who formed a Cristero battalion.

El Santuario de la Virgen de Jalpa, a church nestled on a high ridge above Jovita's pueblo in Jalpa, Zacatecas. Originally an Indigenous temple to an unknown Caxcan goddess, it is now a pilgrimage site honoring La Virgen de Guadalupe and a cornerstone of Catholics in the surrounding region.

she had the support of the surrounding community, who organized supplies of food, weapons, and money. Jovita's remarkable skill set — intelligence, knowledge of the countryside, and keen war strategy — not only kept her troops safe during the six years she fought in the Cristero Revolution, but was key to her own survival as a woman — a woman coronel, no less — in a man's war.

After Jovita surrendered to the Federales in a truce, a Mexican ballad, or corrido, was written in her honor. She received an unexpected pardon plus a sizeable monetary reward from President Lázaro Cárdenas. She used this money to open a successful bar in Jalpa and was known to handle the tough business, often at gunpoint. She enjoyed participating in the local rodeos and betting on horse races. It was said she could lasso a bull to the ground in one fell swoop with her incredible aim while she rode on horseback. She was a joyful and gregarious person who danced with women and men alike. Sometimes, when the mariachi played a favorite, she was so overcome with joy that she'd take her revolver out of its holster and shoot rounds into the air.

As her life progressed, Jovita worked in turns as a maid, a cook, a nanny, a dry cleaner attendant, and an entrepreneur with different businesses across the United States and

Mexico (Chicago, Los Angeles, Nevada, Ciudad Juárez, Jalpa). Despite several proposals of marriage, she refused them all, mostly because the men insisted she wear skirts. She would choose what to wear — and without a doubt, she would wear pants!

She bought property and retired in Jalpa with a pension she received from her years working in the United States. She did not have children but remained very close to her nieces, nephews, and godchildren, in particular Carmen Medina and Teresa de Jesus "Chuy" Ordorica. Chuy was the oldest of five children Jovita helped raise, neighbors who had been temporarily left behind by their seasonal-working mother. Jovita loved them as her own.

In her seventies, she began telling her life's story to her niece Martha Medina, who captured it all on cassette tape. Martha helped Jovita transcribe her stories and collect them into her memoir, *Jovita la Cristera: Una historia viviente*. Jovita wanted to tell her own story, in her own words.

In 1996, at the age of eighty-five, Jovita was diagnosed with cancer, and within a matter of months, she died surrounded by those who loved her.

A traditional adobe home situated in the dry high desert landscape of Zacatecas, the mountainous region in which Jovita fought.

Jovita in her late seventies in Jalpa, Zacatecas, where she retired. Her hair has grown long and is worn braided and wrapped around her head, as was typical of the women during her youth.

Author's note

Jovita Valdovinos was my distant great-aunt. She and my grandfather Jesus Maria "Chema" Viramontes were cousins, and naturally, my mother, Maria Isabel, called her Tía Jovita. Jovita and Chema were very close because he had been a Cristero with Jovita. As a child in Mexico, my mother would sit near them and listen to the many stories they shared during Jovita's visits from El Norte. My mother says that Jovita was a "gran señora," a "great lady," and that while she was relatively small in stature, her presence was as large as the Mexican mesquite tree under which they sat when she visited.

The information in this book is taken primarily from Jovita's memoir, as well as from anecdotes and personal interviews. No person is entirely good or bad, and Jovita's life was as rich as it was complex. In the interviews I conducted with people who knew Jovita, or whose parents or grandparents knew her, many stories emerged in which she was villain and savior alike. The fight for religious freedom in Mexico left some open wounds that linger today. But throughout, there is one constant — Jovita's courage. She was a woman ahead of her time — a feminist, a leader, unconventional, daring, determined, angry, loving, and loyal. She defiantly turned her country's cultural patriarchy on its head. Journalists and historians have referred to Jovita as "Mexico's Joan of Arc," after the young French Catholic woman who also dressed as a man and fought for her country and who was canonized in 1925 at the launch of the Cristero war.

I chose the theme of Jovita wearing pants, something rural women were forbidden to do in the 1920s and '30s, as a symbol of her defiance. There is a Mexican saying that defines Jovita perfectly: "Tiene sus pantalones bien puestos." Literally, it means "they wear their pants well," but symbolically it describes someone with a lot of gumption and valor. Jovita wearing pants was an act of liberation that broke down gender barriers and expectations of women. She would not be stopped. The great courage required to take up arms as a woman remains remarkable today. It is my hope that children, young girls especially, will read Jovita's story and imagine themselves as unstoppable, ferocious, and amazing when they wear pants.

Illustrator's note

When I read Jovita's story, I found myself latching on to her courage, her determination, and the whirlwind that captivated her life. Gentle breezes and turbulent storms; through it all, Jovita pushed on and braved the winds that shaped her into the legend we know of today. I wanted to depict that wild wind in the artwork itself. Whether it was from the gallop of a horse, a cloud over the countryside, the breeze carrying her tears, an explosion of war, the whisper of those lost — I sought to carry that momentum and movement throughout the book itself. Jovita's story is alive, and it breathes with her page to page through Aida's text and, hopefully, through the artwork as well.

For the valiant women of Mexico,
for those from whose revolutionary lineage I descend —
tía, Jovita Valdovinos,
abuelito, Jose Maria "Chema" Viramontes,
mamá, Maria Isabel Viramontes,
and for all those who fight for justice. — A.S.

To all of the courageous women
so close to my heart. — M.M.